A Book of
Prayers

Contents

Introduction

Since the beginning of time, prayer has stood as a powerful pillar of hope binding together people of all backgrounds. Prayer has provided a common language in which to find solace, joy and truth. Its enduring use through the centuries is an absolute testament to the unwavering sanctity of its practice. Whether it is to fervently seek forgiveness, offer praise to a higher power or anything in between, prayer is called upon in an effort to connect with something beyond ourselves.

This anthology is a choice selection, although mainly Christian in origin, representing the myriad of sources of prayer; for prayers do not only find home in religious texts, but also in the hearts and minds of famed poets and inspired thinkers. From the archetypal, influential passages from the Bible and *The Book Common of Prayer*, to the eloquent flow of Sarah Flower Adams' (1805–48) 'Hymn – He Sendeth Sun, He Sendeth Shower', the proliferation of prayer illuminates how, despite conflict and hardship, people have continually found gifts and happiness for which to offer thanks.

Through the words of the historically enlightening leader and priest Martin Luther (1483–1546), prayer calls upon God for fortitude in the face of adversity: in 'From the Depths of Woe I

Raise to Thee', he begs guidance; in 'We Now Implore God the Holy Ghost', he pronounces God's ability to grant mercy.

The versatility and ease of prayer are also qualities that have contributed to its widespread devotion. The form of a prayer can be simple enough for a child to recite, yet retain its sacred meaning; such is the case with 'Now I lay me down to sleep'. However, a prayer can also be poetically effusive like 'Prayer at Sunrise' by James Weldon Johnson (1871–1938), which applauds the splendour of one of God's greatest bestowals: the sun.

Prayer through the medium of song offers an opportunity to honour God through music, as do the many prayer-hymns, some of which are featured in this collection, such as 'Abide with Me' by Henry Francis Lyte (1793–1847) and 'Rock of Ages' by Augustus Montague Toplady (1740–78).

Prayer offers comfort in its continued consistency; it refuses to fade from thought or practice. Featuring prayers from biblical times, through the middle ages, right up to the nineteenth century (including the work of Charles Dickens, 1812–70, and Oscar Wilde, 1854–1900), the twentieth century and the present day, this collection shows just how potent prayer remains.

Divided into six sections, the book journeys from the highest heights of adoration and worship to the passionate plea for the courage to endure in the most trying of times. Whether it is a prayer for peace and love, or any impassioned supplication to a divine being, this anthology offers an engaging read, a chance to reaffirm your faith and an inspiration for reflection.

THANKS & PRAISE

+ HIC Ē DEVS POTĒGISSIMꝰ ꝗP DIVINĀ MAIESTATĒ + SꝰꝰOÏM OPTꝰꝰ ꝗP OVLCEÕS BOITĀGĒ
ꝗꝰ ÎNNERPTOR LIBERALISSIMVS PROPTER IN MĒ
NSÏM LAБꝰꝰ VTVERꝗꝰ

A General Thanksgiving

ALMIGHTY God, Father of all mercies, we thine
unworthy servants do give thee most humble and hearty
thanks for all thy goodness and loving-kindness to us,
and to all men; [*particularly to those who desire now to offer up their
praises and thanksgivings for thy late mercies vouchsafed unto them.*]

We bless thee for our creation, preservation, and all the
blessings of this life; but above all, for thine inestimable
love in the redemption of the world by our Lord Jesus
Christ; for the means of grace, and for the hope of glory.
And, we beseech thee, give us that due sense of all thy
mercies, that our hearts may be unfeignedly thankful,
and that we shew forth thy praise, not only with our
lips, but in our lives; by giving up ourselves to thy
service, and by walking before thee in holiness and
righteousness all our days; through Jesus Christ our
Lord, to whom with thee and the Holy Ghost be all
honour and glory, world without end. Amen.

* *This to be said when any that have been prayed for desire to return praise.*

The Book of Common Prayer, 1662 version

O God! Thou Art My God Alone

O God! Thou art my God alone;
Early to Thee my soul shall cry;
A pilgrim in a land unknown,
A thirsty land whose springs are dry.

O that it were as it hath been,
When praying in the holy place,
Thy power and glory I have seen,
And marked the footsteps of thy grace.

Yet through this rough and thorny maze,
I follow hard on Thee, my God:
Thy hand unseen upholds my ways:
I safely tread where Thou hast trod.

Thee, in the watches of the night,
When I remember on my bed,
Thy presence makes the darkness light;
Thy guardian wings are round my head.

Better than life itself thy love,
Dearer than all beside to me;
For whom have I in heaven above,
Or what on earth, compared with Thee?

Praise with my heart, my mind, my voice,
For all thy mercy I will give:
My soul shall still in God rejoice,
My tongue shall bless Thee while I live.

James Montgomery (1771–1854)

Olney Hymn 36: Afflictions Sanctified By The Word

Oh how I love Thy holy Word,
Thy gracious covenant, O Lord!
It guides me in the peaceful way;
I think upon it all the day.
What are the mines of shining wealth,
The strength of youth, the bloom of health!
What are all joys compared with those
Thine everlasting Word bestows!
Long unafflicted, undismay'd,
In pleasure's path secure I stray'd;
Thou mad'st me feel thy chast'ning rod,
And straight I turned unto my God.
What though it pierced my fainting heart,
I bless'd Thine hand that caused the smart:
It taught my tears awhile to flow,
But saved me from eternal woe.
Oh! hadst Thou left me unchastised,
Thy precepts I had still despised;
And still the snare in secret laid
Had my unwary feet betray'd.
I love Thee, therefore, O my God,
And breathe towards Thy dear abode;
Where, in Thy presence fully blest,
Thy chosen saints for ever rest.

William Cowper (1731–1800)

Hymn – He Sendeth Sun, He Sendeth Shower

He sendeth sun, he sendeth shower,
Alike they're needful for the flower:
And joys and tears alike are sent
To give the soul fit nourishment.
As comes to me or cloud or sun,
Father! thy will, not mine, be done!

Can loving children e'er reprove
With murmurs whom they trust and love?
Creator! I would ever be
A trusting, loving child to thee:
As comes to me or cloud or sun,
Father! thy will, not mine, be done!

Oh, ne'er will I at life repine:
Enough that thou hast made it mine.
When falls the shadow cold of death
I yet will sing, with parting breath,
As comes to me or shade or sun,
Father! thy will, not mine, be done!

Sarah Flower Adams (1805–48)

God

O Thou, who's infinite in space,
Alive in ever-moving matter,
Eternal in the flow of time,
God faceless, with a trinity of faces!
Soul unified and omnipresent,
Who needs no place or reason,
Whom none can ever comprehend,
Whose being permeates all things,
Encompassing, creating, guarding,
Thou, called by us God.

Although a great mind might contrive
To fix the ocean's depths,
To count the sands, the rays of stars,
Thou can't be summed or fixed!
Enlightened souls who have emerged
From your creative light
Cannot begin to grasp your ways:
Our thought alone aspires to thee,
But in your magnitude is lost,
A moment in eternity.

From depths eternal thou invoked
Primordial substances of chaos
Within thine very self thou birthed
Eternity before all time.
And before time from thine self alone
Thou shinest forth within thyself.
All light originates in thee.
Creating all with but a single word
And reaching forth in new creation,
Thou wast, thou art, and thou will ever be!

Thou incarnate the chain of life,
Thou nourish and sustain it.
Thou joinest starts with ends.
Thou bringest life to all through death.
New suns are born from thee
In flowing streams of sparks.
As on a clear and freezing day,
A hoarfrost dusting shines,
And floats, and churns and sparkles,
As do the stars beneath thy vault.

A multitude of shining spheres
Floats off into infinity.
They all fulfil thy laws,
And cast their vivifying rays.
But all these brilliant lanterns–
This mass of glowing crystal–
This roiling crowd of golden waves–
These burning elements–
Or all these gleaming worlds as one–
Compare to thee like night to day.

Compared to thee the earthly realm
Is like a droplet in the sea.
What is this universe I see?
And what am I, compared to thee?
If, in this airy sea, I wish
To multiply a million worlds
By other worlds a hundred times–
Then venture to compare the sum to thee,
All this would be a tiny speck;
So I, compared to thee, am naught.

I'm Naught! But thou shinest through me
With all the splendour of your virtue;
Thou showest yourself through me
Like sun inside a tiny water drop.
I'm Naught! But still I can feel life,
Like something hungering I fly,
I'm always soaring high above.
To be with you is my soul's wish,
It contemplates, reflects and thinks:
If I exist – thou art as well.

Thou art! As nature's order shows,
My heart affirms the same to me,
My reason's sure of it:
Thou art – And I'm no longer naught!
A fraction of the universe's whole,
It seems that I repose in nature's
Critical centre where you started
With the creation of corporeal beasts,
And ended with the heav'nly spirits:
Through me, you fused the chain of life.

I am the link of all existing worlds,
I am the outer brink of matter,
I am the focal point of living things,
I am the starting place of the divine;
Although my flesh rots into ash,
My mind commands the thunderbolts,
I'm king – I'm slave – I'm worm – I'm God!
But though I am miraculous,
Whence did I come?-that no one knows.
I could not by myself have risen.

Creator, I am your invention!
I am a creature of your wisdom.
O, source of life, bestower of blessings,
My soul and king!
According to your iron laws
My self eternal must needs pass
Across the borne of death;
My spirit's clothed in mortal garb
And I return through death alone,
To your eternity – O, father!

Thou art inscrutable, transcendent!
I understand that all my soul's
Imaginings are powerless
Your shadow to describe;
But when thou must be glorified
To pay such tribute we frail men
One course alone can follow.
We venture upwards to thy realm,
To lose ourselves in thy vast otherness
And shed our tears of gratitude.

Gavrila Romanovich Derzhavin (1743–1816)

Sing, My Tongue, The Saviour's Glory

Sing, my tongue, the Saviour's glory,
Of His cross the mystery sing;
Lift on high the wondrous trophy,
Tell the triumph of the King:
He, the world's Redeemer, conquers
Death, through death now vanquishing.

Born for us, and for us given;
Son of man, like us below,
He, as Man with men, abiding
Dwells, the seed of life to sow:
He, our heavy griefs partaking,
Thus fulfils His life of woe.

Word made flesh! His word life-giving,
Gives His flesh our meat to be,
Bids us drink His blood, believing,
Through His death, we life shall see:
Blessed they who thus receiving
Are from death and sin set free.

Low in adoration bending,
Now our hearts our God revere;
Faith, her aid to sight is lending,
Though unseen the Lord is near;
Ancient types and shadows ending,
Christ our paschal Lamb is here.

Praise for ever, thanks and blessing,
Thine, O gracious Father, be:
Praise be Thine, O Christ, who bringeth
Life and immortality.
Praise be Thine, Thou quickening Spirit,
Praise through all eternity.

Thomas Aquinas (1225–74)

For Success (extract)

Lord, behold our family here assembled.
We thank Thee for this place in which we dwell;
for the love that unites us;
for the peace accorded us this day;
for the hope with which we expect the morrow;
for the health, the work, the food, and the bright
    skies, that make our lives delightful;
for our friends in all parts of the earth, and our
    friendly helpers in this foreign isle.

Robert Louis Stevenson (1850–94)

At The Close Of The Year

Let hearts and tongues unite,
And loud thanksgivings raise:
'Tis duty, mingled with delight,
To sing the Saviour's praise.

To him we owe our breath,
He took us from the womb,
Which else had shut us up in death,
And prov'd an early tomb.

When on the breast we hung,
Our help was in the Lord;
'Twas he first taught our infant tongue
To form the lisping word.

When in our blood we lay,
He would not let us die,
Because his love had fix'd a day
To bring salvation nigh.

In childhood and in youth,
His eye was on us still:
Though strangers to his love and truth,
And prone to cross his will.

And since his name we knew,
How gracious has he been:
What dangers has he led us through,
What mercies have we seen!

Now through another year,
Supported by his care,
We raise our Ebenezer here,
'The Lord has help'd thus far'.

Our lot in future years
Unable to foresee,
He kindly, to prevent our fears,
Says, 'Leave it all to me'.

Yea, Lord, we wish to cast
Our cares upon thy breast!
Help us to praise thee for the past,
And trust thee for the rest.

John Newton (1725–1807)

Thanksgiving Prayer

O God, we thank you for this earth, our home;
For the wide sky and the blessed sun,
For the salt sea and the running water,
For the everlasting hills
And the never-resting winds,
For trees and the common grass underfoot.
We thank you for our senses
By which we hear the songs of birds,
And see the splendour of the summer fields,
And taste of the autumn fruits,
And rejoice in the feel of the snow,
And smell the breath of the spring.
Grant us a heart wide open to all this beauty;
And save our souls from being so blind
That we pass unseeing
When even the common thornbush
Is aflame with your glory,
O God our creator,
Who lives and reigns for ever and ever.

Walter Rauschenbusch (1861–1918)

Blessing And Honour And Glory And Power

Blessing and honour and glory and power,
Wisdom and riches and strength evermore
Give ye to Him Who our battle hath won
Whose are the kingdom, the crown, and the throne.

Into the heav'n of the heav'ns hath He gone,
Sitteth He now in the joy of the throne,
Weareth He now of the kingdom the crown,
Singeth He now the new song with His own.

Soundeth the Heaven of the heavens with His Name;
Ringeth the earth with His glory and fame;
Ocean and mountain, stream, forest, and flower
Echo His praises and tell of His power.

Past are the darkness, the storm, and the war,
Come is the radiance, that sparkles afar,
Breaketh the gleam of the day without end,
Riseth the Sun that shall never descend.

Ever ascendeth the song and the joy;
Ever descendeth the love from on high;
Blessing and honour and glory and praise,
This is the theme of the hymns that we raise.

Life of all life, and true Light of all light,
Star of the dawning unchangingly bright,
Sun of the Salem whose light is the Lamb,
Theme of the ever new, ever glad psalm!

Give we the glory and praise to the Lamb;
Take we the robe and the harp and the palm;
Sing we the song of the Lamb that was slain,
Dying in weakness, but rising to reign.

Horatius Bonar (1808–89)

Glory Be To God On High

Glory be to God on high, Alleluia!
Let the whole creation cry, Alleluia!
Peace and blessing He has given, Alleluia!
Earth repeat the songs of heaven, Alleluia!

Creatures of the field and flood, Alleluia!
Earth and sea cry 'God is good', Alleluia!
Toiling pilgrims raise the song, Alleluia!
Saints in light the strain prolong, Alleluia!

Stars that have no voice to sing Alleluia!
Give their glory to our King, Alleluia!
Silent powers and angels' song, Alleluia!
All unto our God belong, Alleluia!

Theodore Chickering Williams (1855–1915)

Doxology

Great God accept our gratitude,
For the great gifts on us bestowed –
For raiment, shelter and for food.

Great God, our gratitude we bring,
Accept our humble offering,
For all the gifts on us bestowed,
Thy name be evermore adored.

Josephine Delphine Henderson Heard (1861–1921)

Hail Father

Hail, Father, whose creating call
Unnumbered worlds attend;
Jehovah, comprehending all,
Whom none can comprehend!

In light unsearchable enthroned,
Whom angels dimly see,
The fountain of the Godhead owned,
And foremost of the Three.

From Thee, through an eternal now,
The Son, Thine offspring, flowed;
An everlasting Father Thou,
An everlasting God.

Nor quite displayed to worlds above,
Nor quite on earth concealed;
By wondrous, unexhausted love,
To mortal man revealed.

Supreme and all-sufficient God,
When nature shall expire,
And worlds created by Thy nod
Shall perish by Thy fire.

Thy Name, Jehovah, be adored
By creatures without end,
Whom none but Thy essential Word
And Spirit comprehend.

Samuel Wesley, Jr. (1690–1739)

All Glory Be To God On High

All glory be to God on high,
Who hath our race befriended!
To us no harm shall now come nigh,
The strife at last is ended;
God showeth His goodwill to men,
And peace shall reign on earth again;
O thank Him for His goodness!

We praise, we worship Thee, we trust
And give Thee thanks forever,
O father, that Thy rule is just
And wise, and changes never;
Thy boundless grace o'er all things reigns,
Thou dost whate'er Thy will ordains;
'Tis well Thou art our Ruler!

O Jesus Christ, our God and Lord,
Begotten of the Father,
O Thou Who hast our peace restored,
And the lost sheep dost gather,
Thou Lamb of God, enthroned on high
Behold our need and hear our cry;
Have mercy on us, Jesus!

O Holy Spirit, precious Gift,
Thou Comforter unfailing,
Do Thou our troubled souls uplift,
Against the foe prevailing;
Avert our woes and calm our dread:
For us the Saviour's blood was shed;
Do Thou in faith sustain us!

Nikolaus Decius (1485–1541)

*Thanksgiving For Deliverance
From The Plague Or Other
Common Sickness*

O LORD God, who hast wounded
us for our sins, and consumed us
for our transgressions, by thy late
heavy and dreadful visitation; and
now, in the midst of judgment
remembering mercy, hast redeemed
our souls from the jaws of death:

We offer unto thy fatherly goodness
ourselves, our souls and bodies
which thou hast delivered, to be
a living sacrifice unto thee, always
praising and magnifying thy
mercies in the midst of thy Church;
through Jesus Christ our Lord.
Amen.

The Book of Common Prayer, 1662 version

Praise God From Whom All Blessings Flow

Praise God from whom all blessings flow;
Praise Him, all creatures here below;
Praise Him above, ye Heavenly Hosts;
Praise Father, Son and Holy Ghost. Amen.

Thomas Ken (1637–1711)

The Song Of Moses

I will sing to the Lord, for he has triumphed gloriously;
    horse and rider he has thrown into the sea.
The Lord is my strength and my might,
    and he has become my salvation;
this is my God, and I will praise him,
    my father's God, and I will exalt him.
The Lord is a warrior;
    the Lord is his name.

Pharaoh's chariots and his army he cast into the sea;
    his picked officers were sunk in the Red Sea.
The floods covered them;
    they went down into the depths like a stone.
Your right hand, O Lord, glorious in power –
    your right hand, O Lord, shattered the enemy
In the greatness of your majesty you overthrew
    your adversaries;
    you sent out your fury, it consumed them like stubble.
At the blast of your nostrils the waters piled up,
    the floods stood up in a heap;
    the deeps congealed in the heart of the sea.
The enemy said, 'I will pursue, I will overtake,
    I will divide the spoil, my desire shall have its fill of them.
    I will draw my sword, my hand shall destroy them'.
You blew with your wind, the sea covered them;
    they sank like lead in the mighty waters.

Who is like you, O Lord, among the gods?
    Who is like you, majestic in holiness,
    awesome in splendour, doing wonders?
You stretched out your right hand,
    the earth swallowed them.

In your steadfast love you led the people whom you redeemed;
    you guided them by your strength to your holy abode.
The peoples heard, they trembled;
    pangs seized the inhabitants of Philistia.
Then the chiefs of Edom were dismayed;
    trembling seized the leaders of Moab;
    all the inhabitants of Canaan melted away.

Terror and dread fell upon them;
    by the might of your arm they became as still as a stone
until your people, O Lord, passed by,
    until the people whom you acquired passed by.
You brought them in and planted them on the mountain of
    your own possession;
    the place, O Lord, that you made your abode,
    the sanctuary, O Lord, that your hands have established.
The Lord will reign forever and ever.

Exodus 15:1–18

Hannah's Prayer

My heart rejoices in the Lord;
    in the Lord my horn is lifted high.
My mouth boasts over my enemies,
    for I delight in your deliverance.

There is no one holy like the Lord;
    there is no one besides you;
    there is no Rock like our God.
Do not keep talking so proudly
    or let your mouth speak such arrogance,
for the Lord is a God who knows,
    and by him deeds are weighed.
The bows of the warriors are broken,
    but those who stumbled are armed with strength.
Those who were full hire themselves out for food,
    but those who were hungry hunger no more.
She who was barren has borne seven children,
    but she who has had many sons pines away.
The Lord brings death and makes alive;
    he brings down to the grave and raises up.

The Lord sends poverty and wealth;
 he humbles and he exalts.
He raises the poor from the dust
 and lifts the needy from the ash heap;
he seats them with princes
 and has them inherit a throne of honour.
For the foundations of the earth are the Lord's;
 upon them he has set the world.

He will guard the feet of his saints,
 but the wicked will be silenced in darkness.
 It is not by strength that one prevails;
those who oppose the Lord will be shattered.
 He will thunder against them from heaven;
the Lord will judge the ends of the earth.
 He will give strength to his king
 and exalt the horn of his anointed.

1 Samuel 2:1–10

David's Song Of Deliverance

The Lord is my rock, my fortress and my deliverer;
    my God is my rock, in whom I take refuge,
my shield and the horn of my salvation.
    He is my stronghold, my refuge and my saviour –
    from violent men you save me.
I call to the Lord, who is worthy of praise,
    and I am saved from my enemies.

The waves of death swirled about me;
    the torrents of destruction overwhelmed me.
The cords of the grave coiled around me;
    the snares of death confronted me.

In my distress I called to the Lord;
    I called out to my God.
From his temple he heard my voice;
    my cry came to his ears.

The earth trembled and quaked,
    the foundations of the heavens shook;
    they trembled because he was angry.
Smoke rose from his nostrils;
    consuming fire came from his mouth,
    burning coals blazed out of it.
He parted the heavens and came down;
    dark clouds were under his feet.
He mounted the cherubim and flew;
    he soared on the wings of the wind.
He made darkness his canopy around him –
    the dark rain clouds of the sky.
Out of the brightness of his presence
    bolts of lightning blazed forth.
The Lord thundered from heaven;
    the voice of the Most High resounded.
He shot arrows and scattered the enemies,
    bolts of lightning and routed them.
The valleys of the sea were exposed
    and the foundations of the earth laid bare
at the rebuke of the Lord,
    at the blast of breath from his nostrils.

He reached down from on high and took hold of me;
    he drew me out of deep waters.
He rescued me from my powerful enemy,
    from my foes, who were too strong for me.

They confronted me in the day of my disaster,
    but the Lord was my support.
He brought me out into a spacious place;
    he rescued me because he delighted in me.

The Lord has dealt with me according to my righteousness;
    according to the cleanness of my hands he has
    rewarded me.
For I have kept the ways of the Lord;
    I have not done evil by turning from my God.
All his laws are before me;
    I have not turned away from his decrees.
I have been blameless before him
    and have kept myself from sin.
The Lord has rewarded me according to my righteousness,
    according to my cleanness in his sight.

To the faithful you show yourself faithful,
    to the blameless you show yourself blameless,
to the pure you show yourself pure,
    but to the crooked you show yourself shrewd.
You save the humble,
    but your eyes are on the haughty to bring them low.
You are my lamp, O Lord;
    the Lord turns my darkness into light.
With your help I can advance against a troop;
    with my God I can scale a wall.

As for God, his way is perfect;
    the word of the Lord is flawless.
    He is a shield
    for all who take refuge in him.

For who is God besides the Lord?
    And who is the Rock except our God?
It is God who arms me with strength
    and makes my way perfect.
He makes my feet like the feet of a deer;
    he enables me to stand on the heights.
He trains my hands for battle;
    my arms can bend a bow of bronze.
You give me your shield of victory;
    you stoop down to make me great.
You broaden the path beneath me,
    so that my ankles do not turn.
I pursued my enemies and crushed them;
    I did not turn back till they were destroyed.
I crushed them completely, and they could not rise;
    they fell beneath my feet.
You armed me with strength for battle;
    you made my adversaries bow at my feet.
You made my enemies turn their backs in flight,
    and I destroyed my foes.
They cried for help, but there was no one to save them –
    to the Lord, but he did not answer.

I beat them as fine as the dust of the earth;
  I pounded and trampled them like mud in the streets.

You have delivered me from the attacks of my people;
  you have preserved me as the head of nations.
  People I did not know are subject to me,
and foreigners come cringing to me;
  as soon as they hear me, they obey me.
They all lose heart;
  they come trembling from their strongholds.

The Lord lives! Praise be to my Rock!
  Exalted be God, the Rock, my Saviour!
He is the God who avenges me,
  who puts the nations under me,
who sets me free from my enemies.
  You exalted me above my foes;
  from violent men you rescued me.

Therefore I will praise you, O Lord, among the nations;
  I will sing praises to your name.
He gives his king great victories;
  he shows unfailing kindness to his anointed,
  to David and his descendants forever.

2 Samuel 22:2–51

Thanksgiving After Childbirth

ALMIGHTY God, we give thee
humble thanks for that thou hast
vouchsafed to deliver this woman thy
servant from the great pain and peril
of Child-birth:

Grant, we beseech thee, most
merciful Father, that she, through
thy help, may both faithfully live,
and walk according to thy will, in
this life present; and also may be
partaker of everlasting glory in the
life to come; through Jesus Christ
our Lord.
Amen.

The Book of Common Prayer, 1662 version

Traditional Prayer

Almighty God,
we thank you for the gift of your holy word.
May it be a lantern to our feet,
a light to our paths,
and a strength to our lives.
Take us and use us
to love and serve all men
in the power of the Holy Spirit
And in the name of your Son,
Jesus Christ our Lord.

Author unknown

Praise For God's Goodness To Israel

Shout with joy to God, all the earth!
    Sing the glory of his name;
    make his praise glorious!
Say to God, 'How awesome are your deeds!
    So great is your power
    that your enemies cringe before you.
All the earth bows down to you;
    they sing praise to you,
    they sing praise to your name'.
    Selah

Come and see what God has done,
    how awesome his works in man's behalf!
He turned the sea into dry land,
    they passed through the waters on foot –
come, let us rejoice in him.
    He rules forever by his power,
his eyes watch the nations –
    let not the rebellious rise up against him.
    Selah

Praise our God, O peoples,
    let the sound of his praise be heard;
he has preserved our lives
    and kept our feet from slipping.
For you, O God, tested us;
    you refined us like silver.
You brought us into prison
    and laid burdens on our backs.
You let men ride over our heads;
    we went through fire and water,
but you brought us to a place of abundance.

I will come to your temple with burnt offerings
    and fulfill my vows to you –
vows my lips promised and my mouth spoke
    when I was in trouble.
I will sacrifice fat animals to you
    and an offering of rams;
I will offer bulls and goats.
    Selah

Come and listen, all you who fear God;
    let me tell you what he has done for me.
I cried out to him with my mouth;
    his praise was on my tongue.
If I had cherished sin in my heart,
    the Lord would not have listened;
but God has surely listened
    and heard my voice in prayer.

Praise be to God,
    who has not rejected my prayer
    or withheld his love from me!

Psalm 66, Attr. King David (1040 BC–970 BC)

A Call To Worship And Obedience

Come, let us sing for joy to the Lord;
    let us shout aloud to the Rock of our salvation.
Let us come before him with thanksgiving
    and extol him with music and song.
For the Lord is the great God,
    the great King above all gods.
In his hand are the depths of the earth,
    and the mountain peaks belong to him.
The sea is his, for he made it,
    and his hands formed the dry land.

Come, let us bow down in worship,
    let us kneel before the Lord our Maker;
for he is our God
    and we are the people of his pasture,
    the flock under his care.

Today, if you hear his voice,
do not harden your hearts as you did at Meribah,
as you did that day at Massah in the desert,
where your fathers tested and tried me,
though they had seen what I did.
For forty years I was angry with that generation;
I said, 'They are a people whose hearts go astray,
and they have not known my ways'.
So I declared on oath in my anger,
'They shall never enter my rest'.

Psalm 95

All Lands Summoned To Praise God

Make a joyful noise to the Lord all the earth.
    Worship the Lord with gladness;
    come into his presence with singing.

Know that the Lord is God.
    It is he that made us and we are his;
    we are his people, and the sheep of his pasture.

Enter his gates with thanksgiving,
    and his courts with praise.
    Give thanks to him, bless his name.

For the Lord is good;
    his steadfast love endures forever,
    and his faithfulness to all generations.

Psalm 100

Thanksgiving For God's Goodness

Praise the Lord, O my soul;
　　all my inmost being, praise his holy name.
Praise the Lord, O my soul,
　　and forget not all his benefits –
who forgives all your sins
　　and heals all your diseases,
who redeems your life from the pit
　　and crowns you with love and compassion,
who satisfies your desires with good things
　　so that your youth is renewed like the eagle's.

The Lord works righteousness
　　and justice for all the oppressed.
He made known his ways to Moses,
　　his deeds to the people of Israel:
The Lord is compassionate and gracious,
　　slow to anger, abounding in love.
He will not always accuse,
　　nor will he harbour his anger forever;
he does not treat us as our sins deserve
　　or repay us according to our iniquities.
For as high as the heavens are above the earth,
　　so great is his love for those who fear him;
as far as the east is from the west,
　　so far has he removed our transgressions from us.

As a father has compassion on his children,
    so the Lord has compassion on those who fear him;
for he knows how we are formed,
    he remembers that we are dust.

As for man, his days are like grass,
    he flourishes like a flower of the field;
the wind blows over it and it is gone,
    and its place remembers it no more.
But from everlasting to everlasting
    the Lord's love is with those who fear him,
    and his righteousness with their children's children –
with those who keep his covenant
    and remember to obey his precepts.

The Lord has established his throne in heaven,
    and his kingdom rules over all.
Praise the Lord, you his angels,
    you mighty ones who do his bidding,
    who obey his word.
Praise the Lord, all his heavenly hosts,
    you his servants who do his will.
Praise the Lord, all his works
    everywhere in his dominion.
Praise the Lord, O my soul.

Psalm 103, Attr. King David (1040 BC–970 BC)

Daniel Blesses God

Blessed be the name of God from age to age,
for wisdom and power are his.
He changes times and seasons,
deposes kings and sets up kings;
he gives wisdom to the wise
and knowledge to those who have understanding.
He reveals deep and hidden things;
he knows what is in the darkness,
and light dwells with him.
To you, O God of my ancestors,
I give thanks and praise,
for you have given me wisdom and power,
and have now revealed to me what we asked of you,
for you have revealed to us what the king ordered.

Daniel 2:20–23

Mary's Song Of Praise or The Magnificat

My soul exalts the Lord,
    And my spirit has rejoiced in God my Saviour.
For He has had regard for the humble state of His
    bondslave;
        For behold, from this time on all generations will
        count me blessed.
For the Mighty One has done great things for me;
    And holy is His name.
And His mercy is upon generation after generation
    toward those who fear Him.
He has done mighty deeds with His arm;
    He has scattered those who were proud in the
    thoughts of their heart.
He has brought down rulers from their thrones,
    And has exalted those who were humble.
He has filled the hungry with good things;
    And sent away the rich empty-handed.
He has given help to Israel His servant,
    In remembrance of His mercy,
As He spoke to our fathers,
    To Abraham and his descendants forever.

Luke 1:46–55

Praise The Judge Of The World

O sing to the Lord a new song,
  For He has done wonderful things,
His right hand and His holy arm have gained the victory
  for Him.
The Lord has made known His salvation;
  He has revealed His righteousness in the sight of the
  nations.
He has remembered His loving kindness and His faithfulness
  to the house of Israel;
All the ends of the earth have seen the salvation of our God.
Shout joyfully to the Lord, all the earth;
  Break forth and sing for joy and sing praises.
Sing praises to the Lord with the lyre,
  With the lyre and the sound of melody.
With trumpets and the sound of the horn
  Shout joyfully before the King, the Lord.
Let the sea roar and all it contains,
  The world and those who dwell in it.
Let the rivers clap their hands,
  Let the mountains sing together for joy
Before the Lord, for He is coming to judge the earth;
He will judge the world with righteousness
  And the peoples with equity.

Psalm 98

Thanksgiving After The Burial Of The Dead

ALMIGHTY God, with whom do live the spirits of them that depart hence in the Lord, and with whom the souls of the faithful, after they are delivered from the burden of the flesh, are in joy and felicity:

We give thee hearty thanks, for that it hath pleased thee to deliver this our brother out of the miseries of this sinful world; beseeching thee, that it may please thee, of thy gracious goodness, shortly to accomplish the number of thine elect, and to hasten thy kingdom; that we, with all those that are departed in the true faith of thy holy Name, may have our perfect consummation and bliss, both in body and soul, in thy eternal and everlasting glory; through Jesus Christ our Lord. Amen.

The Book of Common Prayer, 1662 version

Prayer Of St Richard

Thanks be to Thee, my Lord Jesus Christ
For all the benefits Thou hast given me,
For all the pains and insults Thou hast borne for me.
O most merciful Redeemer, friend and brother,
May I know Thee more clearly,
Love Thee more dearly,
Follow Thee more nearly.

Saint Richard of Chichester (1197–1253)

Thanksgiving For Plenty

O MOST merciful Father,
who of thy gracious goodness
hast heard the devout prayers
of thy Church, and turned our
dearth and scarcity into
cheapness and plenty:

We give thee humble thanks
for this thy special bounty;
beseeching thee to continue
thy loving-kindness unto us,
that our land may yield us her
fruits of increase, to thy glory
and our comfort; through
Jesus Christ our Lord.
Amen.

The Book of Common Prayer,
1662 version

Grace

For what we are about to receive,
May the Lord make us truly thankful.

Traditional, Author unknown

The Selkirk Grace

Some hae meat and canna eat,
and some wad eat that want it,
but we hae meat and we can eat,
and sae the Lord be thankit.

*Traditional Scots poem (often wrongly
attributed to Robert Burns)*

To God Who Gives Our Daily Bread

To God who gives our daily bread
A thankful song we raise,
And pray that he who sends us food
May fill our hearts with praise.

Thomas Tallis (c. 1510–85)

Be Present At Our Table, Lord

Be present at our table, Lord;
Be here and everywhere adored;
Thy creatures bless, and grant that we
May feast in paradise with Thee.

We thank Thee, Lord, for this our food,
For life and health and every good;
By Thine own hand may we be fed;
Give us each day our daily bread.

We thank Thee, Lord, for this our good,
But more because of Jesus' blood;
Let manna to our souls be giv'n,
The Bread of Life sent down from Heav'n.

John Cennick (1718–55)

A *Thanksgiving Day* Prayer

Lord, so often times, as any other day
When we sit down to our meal and pray

We hurry along and make fast the blessing
Thanks, amen. Now please pass the dressing

We're slaves to the olfactory overload
We must rush our prayer before the food gets cold

But Lord, I'd like to take a few minutes more
To really give thanks to what I'm thankful for

For my family, my health, a nice soft bed
My friends, my freedom, a roof over my head

I'm thankful right now to be surrounded by those
Whose lives touch me more than they'll ever possibly know

Thankful Lord, that You've blessed me beyond measure
Thankful that in my heart lives life's greatest treasure

That You, dear Jesus, reside in that place
And I'm ever so grateful for Your unending grace

So please, heavenly Father, bless this food You've provided
And bless each and every person invited

Amen!

Alan Scott Wesemann (b. 1963)

FOR GUIDANCE
AND STRENGTH

The Lord's Prayer

Our Father, who art in heaven,
Hallowed be thy Name.
Thy kingdom come.
Thy will be done,
On earth as it is in heaven.
Give us this day our daily bread.
And forgive us our trespasses,
As we forgive those who trespass against us.
And lead us not into temptation,
But deliver us from evil.
For thine is the kingdom,
and the power, and the glory,
for ever and ever.
Amen.

Based on The Book of Matthew, 6:9-13

The Third Collect, For Grace (Morning Prayer)

O LORD our heavenly Father, Almighty and everlasting God, who hast safely brought us to the beginning of this day:

Defend us in the same with thy mighty power; and grant that this day we fall into no sin, neither run into any kind of danger; but that all our doings being ordered by thy governance, to do always that is righteous in thy sight; through Jesus Christ our Lord.
Amen.

The Book of Common Prayer, 1662 version

The Divine Shepherd

The Lord is my shepherd, I shall not be in want.
    He makes me lie down in green pastures,
he leads me beside quiet waters,
    he restores my soul.
He guides me in paths of righteousness
    for his name's sake.

Even though I walk
    through the valley of the shadow of death,
    I will fear no evil,
for you are with me;
    your rod and your staff,
    they comfort me.

You prepare a table before me
    in the presence of my enemies.
You anoint my head with oil;
    my cup overflows.
Surely goodness and love will follow me
    all the days of my life,
and I will dwell in the house of the Lord
    forever.

Psalm 23, Attr. King David (1040 BC–970 BC)

Hymn

Accept this building, gracious Lord,
No temple though it be;
We raised it for our suffering kin,
And so, Good Lord, for Thee.

Accept our little gift, and give
To all who here may dwell,
The will and power to do their work,
Or bear their sorrows well.

From Thee all skill and science flow;
All pity, care, and love,
All calm and courage, faith and hope,
Oh! pour them from above.

And part them, Lord, to each and all,
As each and all shall need,
To rise like incense, each to Thee,
In noble thought and deed.

And hasten, Lord, that perfect day,
When pain and death shall cease;
And Thy just rule shall fill the earth
With health, and light, and peace.

When ever blue the sky shall gleam,
And ever green the sod;
And man's rude work deface no more
The Paradise of God.

Charles Kingsley (1819–75)

O Lord My God, Receive My Prayer

O Lord my God, receive my prayer
Which is according to thy holy will;
For if, O great king, it should please thee still
I shall defend thee while I still draw air.
Alas, O Lord, I shall backslide once more,
Fatigued too soon unless thy bounty fill
And give resolve unto my own weak will
And with thy virtue open wide the door.
You wish, Lord, to be master of my heart.
Come then O Lord and make me your redoubt
That earthly love and hate be driven out
And good and evil and all care depart.
Only allow me to draw near to you,
Repentant, constant in my faith and true.

Mary Stuart (1542–87)

Psalm Of Protection (extract)

The Lord is my light and my salvation –
    whom shall I fear?
The Lord is the stronghold of my life –
    of whom shall I be afraid?
When evil men advance against me
    to devour my flesh,
when my enemies and my foes attack me,
    they will stumble and fall.
Though an army besiege me,
    my heart will not fear;
though war break out against me,
    even then will I be confident.

Extract from Psalm 27: 1-3,
Attr. King David (1040 bc-970 bc)

Evening Prayer (extract)

Father of Heaven! whose goodness has brought us in safety to the close of this day, dispose our hearts in fervent prayer. Another day is now gone, and added to those, for which we were before accountable. Teach us almighty father, to consider this solemn truth, as we should do, that we may feel the importance of every day, and every hour as it passes, and earnestly strive to make a better use of what thy goodness may yet bestow on us, than we have done of the time past.

Give us grace to endeavour after a truly Christian spirit to seek to attain that temper of forbearance and patience of which our blessed saviour has set us the highest example; and which, while it prepares us for the spiritual happiness of the life to come, will secure to us the best enjoyment of what this world can give. Incline us oh God! to think humbly of ourselves, to be severe only in the examination of our own conduct, to consider our fellow-creatures with kindness, and to judge of all they say and do with that charity which we would desire from them ourselves.

Jane Austen (1775–1817)

Prayer At Sunrise

O mighty, powerful, dark-dispelling sun,
Now thou art risen, and thy day begun.
How shrink the shrouding mists before thy face,
As up thou spring'st to thy diurnal race!
How darkness chases darkness to the west,
As shades of light on light rise radiant from thy crest!
For thee, great source of strength, emblem of might,
In hours of darkest gloom there is no night.
Thou shinest on though clouds hide thee from sight,
And through each break thou sendest down thy light.

O greater Maker of this Thy great sun,
Give me the strength this one day's race to run,
Fill me with light, fill me with sun-like strength,
Fill me with joy to rob the day its length.
Light from within, light that will outward shine,
Strength to make strong some weaker heart than mine,
Joy to make glad each soul that feels its touch;
Great Father of the sun, I ask this much.

James Weldon Johnson (1871–1938)

Celtic Prayer

O God, listen to my prayer
Let my earnest petition come to you,
For I know that you are hearing me
As surely as though I saw you with mine eyes.

I am placing a lock upon my heart,
I am placing a lock upon my thoughts,
I am placing a lock upon my lips
And double-knitting them.

Aught that is amiss for my soul
In the pulsing of my death,
May you, O God, sweep it from me
And may you shield me in the blood of your love.

Let no thought come to my heart,
Let no sound come to my ear,
Let no temptation come to my eye,
Let no fragrance come to my nose,
Let no fancy come to my mind,
Let no ruffle come to my spirit,
That is hurtful to my poor body this night,
Nor ill for my soul at the hour of my death;

But may you yourself, O God of life,
Be at my breast, be at my back,
You to me as a star, you to me as a guide,
From my life's beginning to my life's closing.

Author unknown

Lord Of Our Life, Whom We Fear

Lord of our life, God Whom we fear,
Unknown, yet known; unseen, yet near;
Breath of our breath, in Thee we live;
Life of our life, our praise receive.

Thine eye detects the sparrow's fall;
Thy heart of love expands for all;
Our throbbing life is full of Thee;
Throned in Thy vast infinity.

Shine in our darkness, Light of light,
Our minds illumine, disperse our night;
Make us responsive to Thy will;
Our souls with all Thy fullness fill.

We love Thy Name; we heed Thy rod;
Thy Word our law, O gracious God!
We wait Thy will; on Thee we call:
Our light, our life, our love, our all.

Samuel Francis Smith (1808–95)

*The Collect For The First Sunday
After The Epiphany*

O LORD, we beseech thee mercifully
to receive the prayers of thy people
which call upon thee; and grant that
they may both perceive and know

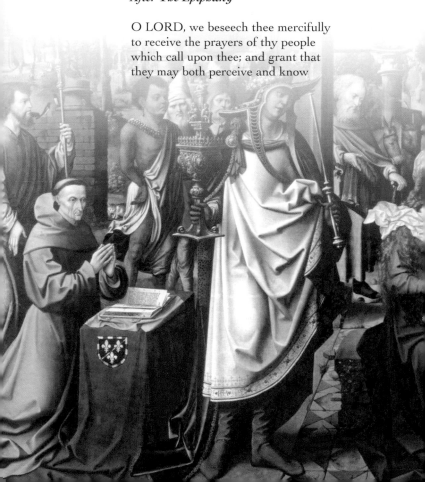

what things they ought to do, and
also may have grace and power
faithfully to fulfil the same; through
Jesus Christ our Lord.
Amen.

The Book of Common Prayer, 1662 version

A Heart

Give me a heart, dear heavenly Father,
a heart that's free of all self-will,
a heart obedient to thy counsel,
that gladly thy commands fulfils.

Give me a heart prepared to practise
true self-denial at any time,
a heart that loves its enemies,
assured of glories yet to come.

Give me a heart of sympathy
for every person mired in sin,
that guides them toward the Father's land,
embraces them, and takes them in.

Give me a heart that hankers not
for worldly pleasures, selfish ends,
a heart that loves the poor, and so
forgets itself, a hand to lend.

Give me a heart that pays no heed
to threats or scorn or ridicule,
that keeps faith always with its God,
though blamed, despised, or called a fool.

A heart like thine, that lives for God –
would such a heart be given to me!
O Jesus, take me and all my gifts:
I'll find this heart alone in thee.

Eberhard Arnold (1883–1935)

From Depths Of Woe I Raise To Thee

From depths of woe I raise to Thee
The voice of lamentation;
Lord, turn a gracious ear to me
And hear my supplication;
If Thou iniquities dost mark,
Our secret sins and misdeeds dark,
O who shall stand before Thee?

To wash away the crimson stain,
Grace, grace alone availeth;
Our works, alas! are all in vain;
In much the best life faileth:
No man can glory in Thy sight,
All must alike confess Thy might,
And live alone by mercy.

Therefore my trust is in the Lord,
And not in mine own merit;
On Him my soul shall rest, His Word
Upholds my fainting spirit:
His promised mercy is my fort,
My comfort, and my sweet support;
I wait for it with patience.

What though I wait the livelong night,
And till the dawn appeareth,
My heart still trusteth in His might;
It doubteth not nor feareth:
Do thus, O ye of Israel's seed,
Ye of the Spirit born indeed;
And wait till God appeareth.

Though great our sins and sore our woes,
His grace much more aboundeth;
His helping love no limit knows,
Our utmost need it soundeth.
Our Shepherd good and true is He,
Who will at last His Israel free.
From all their sin and sorrow.

Martin Luther (1483–1546)

O Everlasting Light

O EVERLASTING Light,
    Giver of dawn and day,
Dispeller of the ancient night
    In which creation lay!

O everlasting Light,
    Shine graciously within!
Brightest of all on earth that's bright,
    Come, shine away my sin!

O everlasting Rock,
    Sole refuge in distress,
My fort when foes assail and mock,
    My rest in weariness!

O everlasting Fount,
    From which the waters burst,
The streams of the eternal mount,
    That quench time's sorest thirst!

O everlasting Health,
  From which all healing springs;
My bliss, my treasure, and my wealth,
  To thee my spirit clings!

O everlasting Truth,
  Truest of all that's true;
Sure guide of erring age and youth,
  Lead me, and teach me too!

O everlasting Strength,
  Uphold me in the way;
Bring me, in spite of foes, at length,
  To joy, and light, and day!

O everlasting Love,
  Wellspring of grace and peace,
Pour down thy fullness from above,
  Bid doubt and trouble cease!

O everlasting Rest,
　　Lift off life's load of care!
Relieve, revive this burthened breast,
　　And every sorrow bear.

Thou art in heaven our all,
　　Our all on earth art thou;
Upon thy glorious name we call,
　　Lord Jesus, bless us now!

Horatius Bonar (1808–89)

Very Bread, Good Shepherd, Tend Us

Very Bread, Good Shepherd, tend us;
Jesu, of Thy love befriend us;
Thou refresh us, Thou defend us,
Thine eternal goodness send us
In the land of life to see:
Thou Who all things canst and knowest,
Who in earth such Food bestowest,
Grant us with Thy saints, though lowest,
Where the heav'nly feast Thou showest,
Fellow heirs and guests to be.

Extract from a translation of
Laud Sion Salvatorem
by Thomas Aquinas (1225–74)

Resource In Temptation

My Saviour! Wilt thou leave me now,
When sharp temptations round me throng?
All other helps have failed – and thou
Alone canst hope and truth prolong.

Tempted; – but can I turn away,
And give my thoughts to aught but thee?
Oh, let me die; but ne'er betray
My pledge of truth and constancy.

I know that sorrow has its power,
I know that pleasure has its charm;
But oft the least propitious hour
Beholds the triumph of thine arm.

Oh, who or what shall lead to sin,
Whate'er its power, whate'er its art –
So long as Christ is King within,
And binds his being round my heart?

Thomas Cogswell Upham (1799–1872)

The Collect For The Eighteenth Sunday After Trinity

LORD, we beseech thee, grant thy people grace to withstand the temptations of the world, the flesh, and the devil, and with pure hearts and minds to follow thee the only God; through Jesus Christ our Lord. Amen.

The Book of Common Prayer, 1662 version

Per Pacem Ad Lucem

I DO not ask, O Lord, that life may be
    A pleasant road;
I do not ask that Thou wouldst take from me
    Aught of its load;

I do not ask that flowers should always spring
    Beneath my feet;
I know too well the poison and the sting
    Of things too sweet.

For one thing only, Lord, dear Lord, I plead,
    Lead me aright –
Though strength should falter, and though heart
    should bleed –
    Through Peace to Light.

I do not ask, O Lord, that thou shouldst shed
  Full radiance here;
Give but a ray of peace, that I may tread
  Without a fear.

I do not ask my cross to understand,
  My way to see;
Better in darkness just to feel Thy hand
  And follow Thee.

Joy is like restless day; but peace divine
  Like quiet night:
Lead me, O Lord, – till perfect Day shall shine,
  Through Peace to Light.

Adelaide Anne Procter (1825–64)

Prayer (extract)

Almighty God, take from me all vain-
glorious minds, all appetites of mine
own praise, all envy, covetise, gluttony,
sloth, and lechery, all wrathful affections,
all appetite of revenging, all desire or
delight of other folk's harm, all pleasure
in provoking any person to wrath and
anger, all delight of exprobation or
insultation against any person in their
affliction and calamity.

And give me, good Lord, an humble,
lowly, quiet, peaceable, patient, charitable,
kind, tender, and pitiful mind with all my
works, and all my words, and all my
thoughts, to have a taste of Thy holy,
blessed Spirit.

Give me, good Lord, a full faith, a firm
hope, and a fervent charity, a love to the
good Lord incomparable above the love
to myself; and that I love nothing to
Thy displeasure, but everything in an
order to Thee.

*Composed by Sir Thomas More (1478–1535)
after being condemned to death*

O Holy Saviour, Friend Unseen

O Holy Saviour, Friend unseen,
Since on Thine arm Thou bid'st us lean,
Help us throughout life's changing scene
By faith to cling to Thee.

When far from home, fatigued, oppressed,
In Thee we found our place of rest;
As exiles still, yet richly blest,
We cling, O Lord, to Thee.

What though the world deceitful prove,
And earthly friends and hopes remove!
With patient, uncomplaining love,
Still would we cling to Thee.

Though faith and hope are often tried,
We ask not, need not, ought beside;
So safe, so calm, so satisfied,
The soul that clings to Thee.

Blest is our lot, whate'er befall;
What can disturb or who appal?
Thou art our strength, our rock, our all,
Saviour, we cling to Thee.

Charlotte Elliott (1789–1871)

My God, Thy Suppliant Hear

My God, thy suppliant hear:
Afford a gentle ear:
For I am comfortless,
And labour in distress.

Thy servant, Lord, defend,
Whose hopes on Thee depend:
From wasting sorrow free
The heart long vowed to Thee.

For Thou art God alone,
To tender pity prone,
Propitious unto all
Who on thy mercy call.

But, O Thou King of kings,
From whom sweet mercy springs, –
Then ready to be found
When troubles most abound, –

O hear my fervent prayer,
And take me to thy care;
Direct me in thy way;
So shall I never stray.

George Sandys (1578–1644)

Jesus, My Saviour, Look On Me

Jesus, my Saviour, look on me,
For I am weary and oppressed;
I come to cast myself on Thee:
Thou art my Rest.

Look down on me, for I am weak;
I feel the toilsome journey's length;
Thine aid omnipotent I seek:
Thou art my Strength.

I am bewildered on my way,
Dark and tempestuous is the night;
O send Thou forth some cheering ray:
Thou art my Light.

I hear the storms around me rise;
But when I dread th'impending shock,
My spirit to the Refuge flies:
Thou art my Rock.

Standing alone on Jordan's brink,
In that tremendous latest strife,
Thou will not suffer me to sink:
Thou art my Life.

Thou wilt my every want supply,
E'en to the end, whate'er befall;
Through life, in death, eternally,
Thou art my All.

Charlotte Elliot (1789–1871)

Jewish Prayer

May God be with me and with his messenger
    whom he has sent to greet me and lead me
    to heaven.

May the Lord who is great and blessed look
    upon me, have pity on me and grant me
    peace.

May he give me greater strength and courage
    that I may not be fearful or afraid.

For the angels of God are about me and God
    is with me wherever I may be.

Author unknown

The Serenity Prayer

God, grant me the serenity
To accept the things I cannot change;
The courage to change the things that I can;
And the wisdom to know the difference.

Based on words by Reinhold Niebuhr (1892–1971)

*A Prayer For Blessing, Direction, Help, And ood Success,
In Any great Enterprise (extract)*

O Lord God, infinitely wise and good, who teachest
man knowledge, and givest both the skill and power to
accomplish our purposes; I know not what to do; but
mine eyes are upon thee; and all my expectation is from
thee: and I desire continually to wait, and call, and
depend upon thee. It is a great work which I have now
to do: but O how little strength have I to do it. All my
sufficiency is of thee, who workest in us to will and to
do of thy good pleasure. Thou that hast been my help,
leave me not, nor forsake me, O God of my salvation;
but let me be taught of God, what I have to do: and let
the gracious Lord make me to understand what is thy
pleasure concerning me. O that my ways were directed
to please thee; that so I might have the light of thy
countenance ever shining upon me!

*Benjamin Jenks (1648–1724), 'altered and improved'
by Rev. Charles Simeon, 1838*

Abide With Me

Abide with me; fast falls the eventide;
the darkness deepens; Lord, with me abide.
When other helpers fail and comforts flee,
Help of the helpless, O abide with me.

Swift to its close ebbs out life's little day;
earth's joys grow dim; its glories pass away;
change and decay in all around I see;
O thou who changest not, abide with me.

I need thy presence every passing hour.
What but thy grace can foil the tempter's power?
Who, like thyself, my guide and stay can be?
Through cloud and sunshine, Lord, abide with me.

I fear no foe, with thee at hand to bless;
ills have no weight, and tears no bitterness.
Where is death's sting? Where, grave, thy victory?
I triumph still, if thou abide with me.

Hold thou thy cross before my closing eyes;
shine through the gloom and point me to the skies.
Heaven's morning breaks, and earth's vain shadows flee;
in life, in death, O Lord, abide with me.

Henry Francis Lyte (1793–1847)

Prayer For Guidance

O gracious and holy Father,
give us wisdom to perceive you,
diligence to seek you,
patience to wait for you,
eyes to behold you,
a heart to meditate upon you,
and a life to proclaim you,
through the power of the Spirit
of Jesus Christ our Lord.
Amen.

Attributed to Saint Benedict of Nursia (480–c. 550)

Teach Us To Master Flesh And Blood

Lord! Make our heart Thy temple in which Thou wouldst live. Grant that every impure thought, every earthly desire might be like the idol Dagon – each morning broken at the feet of the Ark of the Covenant. Teach us to master flesh and blood and let this mastery of ourselves be our bloody sacrifice in order that we might be able to say with the Apostle: 'I die every day'.

Søren Aabye Kierkegaard (1813–55)

PRAYERS FOR
FORGIVENESS

A Child's Hymn

Hear my prayer, O heavenly Father,
Ere I lay me down to sleep;
Bid Thy angels, pure and holy,
Round my bed their vigil keep.

My sins are heavy, but Thy mercy
Far outweighs them, every one;
Down before Thy cross I cast them,
Trusting in Thy help alone.

Keep me through this night of peril
Underneath its boundless shade;
Take me to Thy rest, I pray Thee,
When my pilgrimage is made.

None shall measure out Thy patience
By the span of human thought;
None shall bound the tender mercies
Which Thy Holy Son has bought.

Pardon all my past transgressions,
Give me strength for days to come;
Guide and guard me with Thy blessing
Till Thy angels bid me home.

Charles Dickens (1812–70)

Evening Hymn

O God, whose daylight leadeth down
Into the sunless way,
Who with restoring sleep dost crown
The labour of the day!

What I have done, Lord, make it clean
With thy forgiveness dear;
That so to-day what might have been,
To-morrow may appear.

And when my thought is all astray,
Yet think thou on in me;
That with the new-born innocent day
My soul rise fresh and free.

Nor let me wander all in vain
Through dreams that mock and flee;
But even in visions of the brain,
Go wandering toward thee.

George MacDonald (1824–1905)

Penitence

Great God!
Greater than Greatest! Better than the best!
Kinder than kindest! With soft pity's eye,
... Look down – down – down,
On a poor breathing particle in dust!
Or, lower, – an immortal in his crimes.
His crimes forgive! Forgive his virtues, too!
Those smaller faults, half-converts to the right.

Adapted extract from **The Consolation,**
by Edward Young (1683–1765)

A Prayer

When I look back upon my life nigh spent,
Nigh spent, although the stream as yet flows on,
I more of follies than of sins repent,
Less for offence than Love's shortcomings moan.
With self, O Father, leave me not alone –
Leave not with the beguiler the beguiled;
Besmirched and ragged, Lord, take back thine own:
A fool I bring thee to be made a child.

George MacDonald (1824–1905)

A Complaint Of A Sinner

O Lord most deare, [with] many a teare, lamenting, lame[n]ting,
   I fall before thy face,
And for e[a]ch crime, done ere this time, repenting, repenting
     Most humbly call for grace.
Through wanton will, I must confesse,
Thy precepts still I doe transgresse,
The world with his vayne pleasure,
Bewitcht my senses so,
That I could find no leasure,
   My vices to forgoe.
I graunt I haue through my deserte,
Deserud great plagues and bitter smart.

But yet sweet God, doe stay thy rod, forgeue me, forgeue me,
   Which doe thine ayde implore,
O cease thine ire, I thee desire, beleeue me, beleue me,
   I will so sinne no more.
But still shall pray thy holy name,
   In the right way my steppes to frame,
So shall I not displease thee,
   Which art my Lord of might.
My heart and tongue shall prayse thee,
   Most humbly day and night.
I will delight continually,
   Thy name to lawde and magnify.

With sighes & sobs, my heart it throbs,
    remembring, remembring
    The fraylty of my youth,
I ran a race, deuoyd of grace, not rendring,
    not rendring
    Due reuerence to thy truth.
Such care I cast on earthly toyes,
    That nought I past for heauenly ioyes,
But now it me repenteth,
    My heart doeth bleede for woe,
Which inwardly lamenteth,
    That euer it sinned so.
With many a sigh, and many a grone,
    O Lord to thee I make my mone.

Though furious fires of fond desires, allure
    me, allure me,
    From thee so wander wyde:
Let pitifull eyes, and moystened eyes,
    procure thee, procure thee
    To be my Lorde and guyde.
As Scripture sayth, thou doest not craue,
    A sinners death, but wouldest him saue:
That sinfull wretch am I O Lorde,
    Which would repent and liue,
With ceaslesse plaints I cry Lorde,
    Thy pardon to me geue.
O Lord for thy sweete Iesu sake,
    Doe not shut vp thy mercie gate.

Mercy, mercy, mercy, graunt me I pray
   thee, I pray thee,
    Graunt mercy louing Lorde,
Let not the Diuel which meanes me euill,
   betray me, betray mee,
    Protect me with thy worde.
So shall my heart find sweete reliefe,
   Which now feeles smart and bitter griefe,
O Lord, I doe request thee,
   To guyde my steppes so well,
That when death shall arest me,
   My soule with thee may dwell
In heauen aboue, where Angels sing,
   Continuall prayse, to thee theyr king.

Humfrey Gifford (1550–1600)

A Hymn To God The Father

Wilt thou forgive that sin where I begun,
    Which was my sin, though it were done before?
Wilt thou forgive that sin, through which I run,
    And do run still: though still I do deplore?
        When thou hast done, thou hast not done,
          For I have more.

Wilt thou forgive that sin which I have won
    Others to sin? and made my sin their door?
Wilt thou forgive that sin which I did shun
    A year, or two, but wallow'd in, a score?
        When thou hast done, thou hast not done,
          For I have more.

I have a sin of fear, that when I have spun
    My last thread, I shall perish on the shore
But swear by thyself, that at my death thy Son
    Shall shine as he shines now, and heretofore;
        And, having done that, thou hast done,
          I fear no more.

John Donne (1572–1631)

Prayer For Cleansing And Pardon

Have mercy on me, O God,
    according to your unfailing love;
according to your great compassion
    blot out my transgressions.
Wash away all my iniquity
    and cleanse me from my sin.

For I know my transgressions,
    and my sin is always before me.
Against you, you only, have I sinned
    and done what is evil in your sight,
so that you are proved right when you speak
    and justified when you judge.
Surely I was sinful at birth,
    sinful from the time my mother conceived me.

Surely you desire truth in the inner parts;
    you teach me wisdom in the inmost place.
Cleanse me with hyssop, and I will be clean;
    wash me, and I will be whiter than snow.
Let me hear joy and gladness;
    let the bones you have crushed rejoice.
Hide your face from my sins
    and blot out all my iniquity.

Create in me a pure heart, O God,
    and renew a steadfast spirit within me.
Do not cast me from your presence
    or take your Holy Spirit from me.
Restore to me the joy of your salvation
    and grant me a willing spirit, to sustain me.
Then I will teach transgressors your ways,
    and sinners will turn back to you.
Save me from bloodguilt, O God,
    the God who saves me,
    and my tongue will sing of your righteousness.

O Lord, open my lips,
    and my mouth will declare your praise.
You do not delight in sacrifice, or I would bring it;
    you do not take pleasure in burnt offerings.
The sacrifices of God are a broken spirit;
    a broken and contrite heart,
    O God, you will not despise.

In your good pleasure make Zion prosper;
    build up the walls of Jerusalem.
Then there will be righteous sacrifices,
    whole burnt offerings to delight you;
    then bulls will be offered on your altar.

Psalm 51, Attr. King David (1040 BC–970 BC)

An Evening Prayer

All praise to Thee, my God, this night,
For all the blessings of the light!
Keep me, O keep me, King of kings,
Beneath Thine own almighty wings.

Forgive me, Lord, for Thy dear Son,
The ill that I this day have done,
That with the world, myself, and Thee,
I, ere I sleep, at peace may be.

Teach me to live, that I may dread
The grave as little as my bed.
Teach me to die, that so I may
Rise glorious at the judgment day.

O may my soul on Thee repose,
And with sweet sleep mine eyelids close,
Sleep that may me more vigorous make
To serve my God when I awake.

When in the night I sleepless lie,
My soul with heavenly thoughts supply;
Let no ill dreams disturb my rest,
No powers of darkness me molest.

O when shall I, in endless day,
For ever chase dark sleep away,
And hymns divine with angels sing,
All praise to thee, eternal King?

Praise God, from Whom all blessings flow;
Praise Him, all creatures here below;
Praise Him above, ye heavenly host;
Praise Father, Son, and Holy Ghost.

Thomas Ken (1637–1711)

Prayer For Forgiveness Of Sins

My Jesus, I place all my sins before you.
In my estimation
They do not deserve pardon,
But I ask you
To close your eyes
To my want of merit
And open them
To your infinite merit.

Since you willed
To die for my sins,
Grant me forgiveness
For all of them.
Thus, I may no longer feel
The burden of my sins,
A burden that oppresses me
Beyond measure.

Assist me, dear Jesus,
For I desire to become good
No matter what the cost
Take away, destroy,
And utterly root out
Whatever you find in me
That is contrary
To your holy will.
At the same time, dear Jesus, illumine me
So that I may walk in your holy light.

Saint Gemma Galgani (1878–1903)

The Prayer Of Saint Ephrem

O Lord and Master of my life, give me not the spirit
of sloth, idle curiosity, lust for power and idle talk.

But grant unto me, Thy servant, a spirit of chastity,
humility, patience and love.

Yea, O Lord and King, grant me to see mine own
faults and not to judge my brother. For blessed art
Thou unto the ages of ages. Amen.

Written in the name of Saint Ephrem (c. 306–373)

A Confession For Morning Prayer

Almighty and most merciful Father,
We have erred, and strayed from thy ways
    like lost sheep,
We have followed too much the devices and
    desires of our own hearts,
We have offended against thy holy laws,
We have left undone those things which we
    ought to have done,
And we have done those things which we
    ought not to have done,
And there is no health in us:
But thou, O Lord, have mercy upon us,
    miserable offenders;
Spare thou them, O God, which confess
    their faults.
Restore thou them that are penitent;
According to thy promises declared unto
    mankind in Christ Jesu our Lord:
And grant, O most merciful Father, for his sake,
That we may hereafter live a godly, righteous,
    and sober life,
To the glory of thy holy Name.
Amen.

The Book of Common Prayer, 1662

The Collect for Ash Wednesday

ALMIGHTY and everlasting God, who hatest nothing that thou hast made and dost forgive the sins of all them that are penitent:

Create and make in us new and contrite hearts, that we, worthily lamenting our sins, and acknowledging our wretchedness, may obtain of thee, the God of all mercy, perfect remission and forgiveness; through Jesus Christ our Lord. Amen.

The Book of Common Prayer, 1662

Coventry Litany Of Reconciliation

All have sinned and fallen short of the
  glory of God.

The hatred which divides nation from
  nation, race from race, class from class,
Father Forgive.

The covetous desires of people and nations
  to possess what is not their own,
Father Forgive.

The greed which exploits the work of
  human hands and lays waste the earth,
Father Forgive.

Our envy of the welfare and happiness
of others,
Father Forgive.

Our indifference to the plight of the
imprisoned, the homeless, the refugee,
Father Forgive.

The lust which dishonours the bodies of
men, women and children,
Father Forgive.

The pride which leads us to trust in
ourselves and not in God,
Father Forgive.

Be kind to one another, tender-hearted,
forgiving one another, as God in Christ
forgave you.

Coventry Cathedral, post-1940

Extract From Prayers For 'Saturday Morning'

O merciful Father, regard not what we have done against thee;
but what our blessed Saviour hath done for us. Regard not what
we have made ourselves, but what He is made unto us of thee, our
GOD. O that Christ may be to every one of our souls, 'wisdom
and righteousness, sanctification and redemption'; that his precious
blood may cleanse us from all our sins; and that thy Holy Spirit
may renew and sanctify our souls. May He crucify our flesh with
its affections and lusts, and mortify all our members which are
upon earth. O let not 'sin reign in our mortal bodies, that we
should obey it in the lusts thereof'; but, 'being made free from sin,
let us be the servants of righteousness'. Let us approve our hearts
to thee, and let all our ways be pleasing in thy sight.

John Wesley (1703–91)

An Evening Prayer

If I have wounded any soul today,
If I have caused one foot to go astray,
If I have walked in my own willful way,
Dear Lord, forgive!

If I have uttered idle words or vain,
If I have turned aside from want or pain,
Lest I myself shall suffer through the strain,
Dear Lord, forgive!

If I have been perverse or hard, or cold,
If I have longed for shelter in Thy fold,
When Thou hast given me some fort to hold,
Dear Lord, forgive!

Forgive the sins I have confessed to Thee;
Forgive the secret sins I do not see;
O guide me, love me and my keeper be,
Dear Lord, Amen.

C. Maude Battersby (c. 1911)

Rock Of Ages

Rock of Ages, cleft for me,
Let me hide myself in Thee;
Let the water and the blood,
From Thy wounded side which flowed,
Be of sin the double cure;
Save from wrath and make me pure.

Not the labour of my hands
Can fulfil Thy law's demands;
Could my zeal no respite know,
Could my tears forever flow,
All for sin could not atone;
Thou must save, and Thou alone.

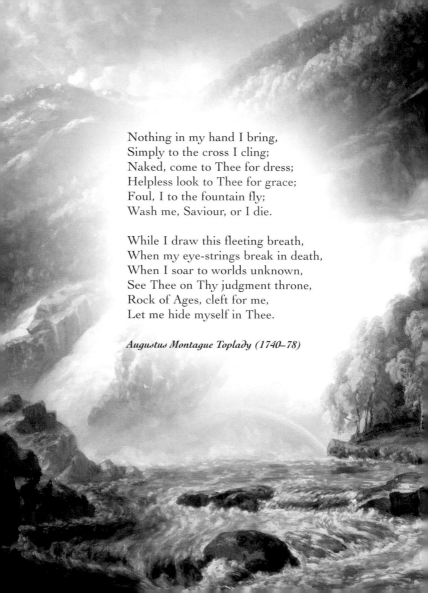

Nothing in my hand I bring,
Simply to the cross I cling;
Naked, come to Thee for dress;
Helpless look to Thee for grace;
Foul, I to the fountain fly;
Wash me, Saviour, or I die.

While I draw this fleeting breath,
When my eye-strings break in death,
When I soar to worlds unknown,
See Thee on Thy judgment throne,
Rock of Ages, cleft for me,
Let me hide myself in Thee.

Augustus Montague Toplady (1740–78)

Confession Of Sin

Father, I have sinned against Thee, and am not worthy to be called Thy child; but I come to Thee. Father, I hate myself; but Thou lovest me. I do not understand myself; but Thou dost, and Thou wilt be merciful to the work of Thine own hands. I cannot guide and help myself, but Thou canst help me, and Thou wilt too, because Thou art my Father, and nothing can part me from Thy love, or from the love of Thy Son, my King. I come and claim my share in Thee, just because I have nothing, and can bring Thee nothing, but lie at Thy gate as a beggar full of sores, desiring to be fed with the crumbs from Thy table. And if I would help the wretched, how much more wilt Thou help me. Thy name is Love, and Thy glory is the likeness of Thy Son Jesus Christ, who said, 'Come to me, all ye that are weary and heavy laden, and I will give you rest'; 'If ye being evil know how to give good gifts to your children, how much more shall your heavenly Father give His Holy Spirit to them that ask Him'.
Amen.

Charles Kingsley (1819–75)

FOR PEACE, LOVE
AND FELLOW MAN

The Second Collect For Peace (Morning Prayer)

O GOD who art the author of peace and lover of concord, in knowledge of whom standeth our eternal life, whose service is perfect freedom:

Defend us thy humble servants in all assaults of our enemies that we, surely trusting in thy defence, may not fear the power of any adversaries, through the might of Jesus Christ our Lord.
Amen.

The Book of Common Prayer, 1662 version

Grant Us Your Peace

O Lord, my God,
grant us your peace; already, indeed,
   you have made us rich in all things!
Give us that peace of being at rest,
that sabbath peace,
the peace which knows no end.

Saint Augustine of Hippo (354–430)

Pax Christi Daily Prayer

Thank you loving God
For the gift of life
For this wonderful world which we all share
For the joy of love and friendship
For the challenge of helping to build
    your kingdom.

Strengthen
My determination to work for a world of peace
    and justice
My conviction that, whatever our nationality or
    race, we are all global citizens, one in Christ
My courage to challenge the powerful with the
    values of the Gospel
My commitment to find nonviolent ways of
    resolving conflict – personal, local, national
    and international
My efforts to forgive injuries and to love those
    I find it hard to love.

Teach me
To share the gifts you have given me
To speak out for the victims of injustice who
  have no voice
To reject the violence which runs through
  much of our world today.

Holy Spirit of God
Renew my hope for a world free from the
  cruelty and evil of war so that we may all
  come to share in God's peace and justice.
Amen

Pax Christi International Catholic Movement for Peace

Let Us Pray

Let us pray for those who foster violence,
those who do not forgive others.
May the Lord change their hearts,
that they may seek peace
and love their brothers and sisters

Author unknown, Ivory Coast

Hush, All Ye Sounds Of War

Hush, all ye sounds of war, ye nations all be still,
A voice of heav'nly joy steals over vale and hill,
O hear the angels sing the captive world's release,
This day is born in Bethlehem the Prince of Peace.

No more divided be, ye families of men,
Old enmity forget, old friendship knit again,
In the new year of God let brothers' love increase,
This day is born in Bethlehem the Prince of Peace.

William H. Draper (1855–1933)

God's Defence Of His City And People

God is our refuge and strength,
    an ever-present help in trouble.
Therefore we will not fear, though the earth give way
    and the mountains fall into the heart of the sea,
though its waters roar and foam
    and the mountains quake with their surging.
                                         Selah

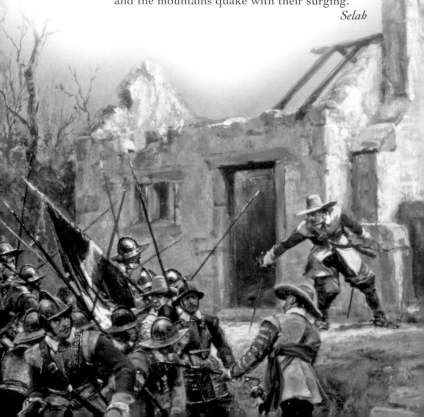

There is a river whose streams make glad the city of God,
the holy place where the Most High dwells.
God is within her, she will not fall;
God will help her at break of day.
Nations are in uproar, kingdoms fall;
he lifts his voice, the earth melts.
The Lord Almighty is with us;
the God of Jacob is our fortress.

Selah

Come and see the works of the Lord,
the desolations he has brought on the earth.
He makes wars cease to the ends of the earth;
he breaks the bow and shatters the spear,
he burns the shields with fire.
'Be still, and know that I am God;
I will be exalted among the nations,
I will be exalted in the earth.'
The Lord Almighty is with us;
the God of Jacob is our fortress.

Selah

Psalm 46

Turn Our Hearts

To you, O Son of God, Lord Jesus Christ,
as you pray to the eternal Father,
we pray, make us one in him.
Lighten our personal distress
and that of our society.
Receive us into the fellowship
of those who believe.
Turn our hearts, O Christ,
to truth everlasting
and healing harmony.

Philip Melanchthon (1497–1560)

To Do Our Part

God our Father, Creator of the world,
please help us to love one another.
Make nations friendly with other nations;
make all of us love one another like brothers and sisters.
Help us to do our part to bring peace in the world
and happiness to all people.

Author unknown, Japanese

When You Sit Happy In Your Own Fair House

When you sit happy in your own fair house,
Remember all poor men who are abroad,
That Christ, who gave this roof, prepare for thee
Eternal dwelling in the house of God.

Alcuin of York (730s or 740s–804)

Messiah, Prince Of Peace!

Messiah, Prince of peace!
Where men each other tear,
Where war is learned, they must confess,
Thy kingdom is not there.
Who, prompted by Thy foe,
Delight in human blood,
Apollyon is their king, we know,
And Satan is their god.

But shall he still devour
The souls redeemed by Thee?
Jesus, stir up Thy glorious power
And end the apostasy!
Come, Saviour, from above,
O'er all our hearts to reign;
And plant the kingdom of Thy love
In every heart of man.

Then shall we exercise
The hellish art no more,
While Thou our long-lost paradise
Dost with Thyself restore.
Fightings and wars shall cease,
And, in Thy Spirit giv'n,
Pure joy and everlasting peace
Shall turn our earth to Heav'n.

John and Charles Wesley (1703–91 and 1707–88)

In The Time Of War And Tumults

O ALMIGHTY God, King of all kings, and Governor of all things, whose power no creature is able to resist, to whom it belongeth justly to punish sinners, and to be merciful to them that truly repent:

Save and deliver us, we humbly beseech thee, from the hands of our enemies; abate their pride, asswage [sic] their malice, and confound their devices; that we, being armed with thy defence, may be preserved evermore from all perils, to glorify thee, who art the only giver of all victory; through the merits of thy Son, Jesus Christ our Lord. Amen.

The Book of Common Prayer, 1662 version

The Collect For Saint Stephen's Day

GRANT, O Lord, that, in all our sufferings here upon earth, for the testimony of thy truth, we may stedfastly [sic] look up to heaven, and by faith behold the glory that shall be revealed; and, being filled with the Holy Ghost, may learn to love and bless our persecutors, by the example of thy first Martyr Saint Stephen, who prayed for his murderers to thee, O blessed Jesus, who standest at the right hand of God to succour all those that suffer for thee, our only Mediator and Advocate. Amen.

The Book of Common Prayer, 1662 version

An Interfaith Prayer For Peace

O God, you are the source of life and peace.
Praised be your name forever.
We know it is you who turn our minds to thoughts
  of peace.
Hear our prayer in this time of crisis.
Your power changes hearts
Muslims, Christians and Jews remember, and
  profoundly affirm,
That they are followers of the one God,
Children of Abraham, brothers and sisters;
Enemies begin to speak to one another;

those who were estranged join hands in friendship;
nations seek the way of peace together.
Strengthen our resolve to give witness to these
truths by the way we live.

Give to us:
Understanding that puts an end to strife;
Mercy that quenches hatred, and
Forgiveness that overcomes vengeance.

Empower all people to live in your law of love
Amen.

Author unknown, Pax Christi

Give Peace In These Our Days, O Lord

Give peace in these our days, O Lord,
Great dangers are now at hand;
Thine enemies with one accord
Christ's Name in every land
Seek to deface, root out and rase,
Thy true right worship indeed.
Be Thou the Stay, O Lord, we Thee pray.
Thou helpest alone in all need.

Give us that peace that we do lack,
Through misbelief, and in ill life.
Thy Word to offer Thou dost not slack,
Which we unkindly gainstrive.
With fire and sword, this healthful Word
Some persecute and oppress.
Some with the mouth confess the truth
Without sincere godliness.

Give peace and us Thy sprite down send
With grief and repentance true;
Do piece our hearts our lives to amend,
And by faith Christ renew;
That fear and dread, war and bloodshed,
Through Thy sweet mercy and grace,
May from us slide, Thy truth abide,
And shine in every place.

*Wolfgang Köpfel (1478–1541), translated from German
to English by Edmund Grindal (1519–83)*

Prayer Of St Francis

Lord, make me an instrument of your Peace
Where there is hatred, let me sow love.
Where there is injury, pardon.
Where there is doubt, faith.
Where there is despair, hope.
Where there is darkness, light.
Where there is sadness, joy.

O Divine Master, grant that I may not so much seek
To be consoled as to console;
To be understood, as to understand;
To be loved, as to love;
For it is in giving that we receive,
It is in pardoning that we are pardoned
And it is in dying that we are born to Eternal Life.

Original version attr. Saint Francis of Assisi, 13th century

O God Of Love, O King Of Peace

O God of love, O King of Peace,
Make wars throughout the world to cease;
The wrath of sinful men restrain,
Give peace, O God, give peace again!

Prayer For Peace

Send Thy peace, O Lord, which is perfect and everlasting,
    that our souls may radiate peace.
Send Thy peace, O Lord, that we may think, act,
    and speak harmoniously.
Send Thy peace, O Lord, that we may be contented and
    thankful for Thy bountiful gifts.
Send Thy peace, O Lord, that amidst our worldly strife we
    may enjoy thy bliss.
Send Thy peace, O Lord, that we may endure all, tolerate all
    in the thought of thy grace and mercy.
Send Thy peace, O Lord, that our lives may become a divine
    vision, and in Thy light all darkness may vanish.
Send Thy peace, O Lord, our Father and Mother,
    that we Thy children on earth may all unite in one family.
Amen.

Hazrat Pir-o-Murshid Inayat Khan (1882–1927)

Remember, Lord, Thy works of old,
The wonders that our fathers told;
Remember not our sin's dark stain,
Give peace, O God, give peace again!

Whom shall we trust but Thee, O Lord?
Where rest but on Thy faithful Word?
None ever called on Thee in vain,
Give peace, O God, give peace again!

Where saints and angels dwell above,
All hearts are knit in holy love;
O bind us in that heavenly chain!
Give peace, O God, give peace again!

Henry Williams Baker (1821–77)

Collect For Love

Almighty and most merciful Father, Who hast
given us a new commandment that we should love
one another, give us also grace that we may fulfil
it. Make us gentle, courteous, and forbearing.
Direct our lives, so that we may look each to the
good of others in word and deed. And hallow all
our friendships by the blessing of Thy Spirit, for
His sake, who loved us and gave Himself for us,
JESUS CHRIST our Lord. Amen.

Brooke Foss Westcott (1825–1901)

FOR HEALING, MERCY
AND SALVATION

In The Time Of Plague Or Sickness

O ALMIGHTY God, who in thy wrath didst send a plague upon thine own people in the wilderness, for their obstinate rebellion against Moses and Aaron; and also, in the time of king David, didst slay with the plague of Pestilence threescore and ten thousand, and yet remembering thy mercy didst save the rest:

Have pity upon us miserable sinners, who now are visited with great sickness and mortality; that like as thou didst then accept of an atonement, and didst command the destroying Angel to cease from punishing, so it may now please thee to withdraw from us, who humbly acknowledge our sins and truly repent us of them, this plague and grievous sickness; that being delivered we may glorify thy Name, through Jesus Christ our Lord.
Amen.

The Book of Common Prayer, 1662 version

Jesus, In Sickness And In Pain

Jesus, in sickness and in pain,
Be near to succour me,
My sinking spirit still sustain;
To Thee I turn, to Thee.

When cares and sorrows thicken round,
And nothing bright I see,
In Thee alone can help be found;
To Thee I turn, to Thee.

Should strong temptations fierce assail,
As if to ruin me,
Then in Thy strength will I prevail,
While still I turn to Thee.

Through all my pilgrimage below,
Whate'er my lot may be,
In joy or sadness, weal or woe,
Jesus, I'll turn to Thee.

Thomas Gallaudet (1822–1902)

Jesu, Lord Of Life And Glory

Jesu, Lord of life and glory,
Bend from Heav'n Thy gracious ear;
While our waiting souls adore Thee,
Friend of helpless sinners, hear:
By Thy mercy, O deliver us, good Lord.

Taught by Thine unerring Spirit,
Boldly we draw nigh to God,
Only in Thy spotless merit,
Only through Thy precious blood:
By Thy mercy, O deliver us, good Lord.

From the depth of nature's blindness,
From the hardening power of sin,
From all malice and unkindness,
From the pride that lurks within:
By Thy mercy, O deliver us, good Lord.

When temptation sorely presses,
In the day of Satan's power,
In our times of deep distresses,
In each dark and trying hour:
By Thy mercy, O deliver us, good Lord.

When the world around is smiling,
In the time of wealth and ease,
Earthly joys our hearts beguiling,
In the day of health and peace,
By Thy mercy, O deliver us, good Lord.

In the weary hours of sickness,
In the times of grief and pain,
When we feel our mortal weakness,
When the creature's help is vain:
By Thy mercy, O deliver us, good Lord.

In the solemn hour of dying,
In the awful judgment day,
May our souls, on Thee relying,
Find Thee still our Rock and Stay:
By Thy mercy, O deliver us, good Lord.

Jesu, may Thy promised blessing
Comfort to our souls afford;
May we now, Thy love possessing,
And at length our full reward,
Ever praise Thee, Thee, our ever glorious Lord.

James John Cummins (1795–1867)

A Prayer

O Lord, the hard-won miles
    Have worn my stumbling feet:
Oh, soothe me with thy smiles,
    And make my life complete.

The thorns were thick and keen
    Where'er I trembling trod;
The way was long between
    My wounded feet and God.

Where healing waters flow
    Do thou my footsteps lead.
My heart is aching so;
    Thy gracious balm I need.

Paul Laurence Dunbar (1872–1906)

E Tenebris

COME down, O Christ, and help me! reach thy hand,
　　For I am drowning in a stormier sea
　　Than Simon on thy lake of Galilee:
The wine of life is spilt upon the sand,
My heart is as some famine-murdered land,
　　Whence all good things have perished utterly,
　　And well I know my soul in Hell must lie
If I this night before God's throne should stand.
'He sleeps perchance, or rideth to the chase,
　　Like Baal, when his prophets howled that name
　　From morn to noon on Carmel's smitten height.'
Nay, peace, I shall behold before the night,
　　The feet of brass, the robe more white than flame,
　　The wounded hands, the weary human face.

Oscar Wilde (1854–1900)

Prayer For Healing

And God shall wipe away all tears from their eyes;
and there shall be no more death,
neither sorrow, nor crying,
neither shall there be any more pain:
for the former things are passed away.

Revelation 21:4

Holy Father, Hear My Cry

Holy Father, hear my cry;
Holy Saviour, bend Thine ear;
Holy Spirit, come Thou nigh;
Father, Saviour, Spirit, hear.

Father, save me from my sin;
Saviour, I Thy mercy crave;
Gracious Spirit, make me clean:
Father, Saviour, Spirit, save.

Father, let me taste Thy love;
Saviour, fill my soul with peace;
Spirit, come my heart to move:
Father, Son, and Spirit, bless.

Father, Son, and Spirit – Thou
One Jehovah, shed abroad
All Thy grace within me now;
Be my Father and my God.

Horatius Bonar (1808–89)

Spirit Of Holiness, Descend

Spirit of holiness, descend:
Thy people wait for Thee;
Thine ear in kind compassion lend;
Let us Thy mercy see.

Thy light that on our souls hath shone,
Lead us in hope to Thee;
Let us not feel its rays alone,
Alone Thy people be.

O bring our dearest friends to God;
Remember those we love;
Fit them on earth for Thine abode,
Fit them for joys above.

Spirit of holiness, 'tis Thine
To hear our feeble prayer;
Come, for we wait Thy power divine,
Let us Thy mercy share.

Samuel Francis Smith (1808–95)

We Now Implore God The Holy Ghost

We now implore God the Holy Ghost
For the true faith, which we need the most,
That in our last moments He may befriend us
And, as homeward we journey, attend us.
Lord, have mercy!

Shine in our hearts, O most precious Light,
That we Jesus Christ may know aright,
Clinging to our Saviour, Whose blood hath bought us,
Who again to our homeland hath brought us.
Lord, have mercy!

Thou sacred Love, grace on us bestow,
Set our hearts with heav'nly fire aglow
That with hearts united we love each other,
Of one mind, in peace with every brother.
Lord, have mercy!

Thou highest Comfort in every need,
Grant that neither shame nor death we heed,
That e'en then our courage may never fail us
When the foe shall accuse and assail us.
Lord, have mercy!

Martin Luther (1483–1546)

Holy Sonnet I: Thou Hast Made Me

Thou hast made me, and shall thy work decay?
Repair me now, for now mine end doth haste;
I run to death, and death meets me as fast,
And all my pleasures are like yesterday.
I dare not move my dim eyes any way,
Despair behind, and death before doth cast
Such terror, and my feeble flesh doth waste
By sin in it, which it towards hell doth weigh.
Only thou art above, and when towards thee
By thy leave I can look, I rise again;
But our old subtle foe so tempteth me
That not one hour myself I can sustain.
Thy grace may wing me to prevent his art,
And thou like adamant draw mine iron heart.

John Donne (1572–1631)

Prayer For Recovery From Grave Illness

O Lord, do not rebuke me in your anger
    or discipline me in your wrath.
Be merciful to me, Lord, for I am faint;
    O Lord, heal me, for my bones are in agony.
My soul is in anguish.
    How long, O Lord, how long?

Turn, O Lord, and deliver me;
    save me because of your unfailing love.
No one remembers you when he is dead.
    Who praises you from the grave?

I am worn out from groaning;
    all night long I flood my bed with weeping
    and drench my couch with tears.
My eyes grow weak with sorrow;
    they fail because of all my foes.

Away from me, all you who do evil,
    for the Lord has heard my weeping.
The Lord has heard my cry for mercy;
    the Lord accepts my prayer.
All my enemies will be ashamed and dismayed;
    they will turn back in sudden disgrace.

Psalm 6

Supplication For Mercy

To you I lift up my eyes,
   O you who are enthroned in the heavens!
As the eyes of servants
   look to the hand of their master,
as the eyes of a maid
   to the hands of her mistress,
so our eyes look to the Lord our God,
   until he has mercy upon us.

Have mercy upon us, O Lord, have mercy upon us,
   for we have had more than enough of contempt.
Our soul has had more than its fill
   of the scorn of those who are at ease,
   of the contempt of the proud.

Psalm 123

Early Scottish Prayer

Thou who guidest Noah over the flood waves: hear us.
Thou who with thy word recalled Jonah from the deep:
    deliver us.
Thou who stretched forth thy hand to Peter as he sank:
    help us, O Christ.
Son of God, who didst marvellous things of old: be
    favourable in our day also.

Author unknown

The Collect For The Ascension Day

GRANT, we beseech thee, Almighty God, that like as we do believe thy only begotten Son our Lord Jesus Christ to have ascended into the heavens; so we may also in heart and mind thither ascend, and with him continually dwell, who liveth and reigneth with thee and the Holy Ghost, one God, world without end.
Amen.

The Book of Common Prayer, 1662 version

The Collect For The Day Of Saint Luke The Evangelist

ALMIGHTY God, who calledst Luke the Physician, whose praise is in the Gospel, to be an Evangelist, and Physician of the soul:

May it please thee, that, by the wholesome medicines of the doctrine delivered by him, all the diseases of our souls may be healed; through the merits of thy Son Jesus Christ our Lord.
Amen.

The Book of Common Prayer, 1662 version

A Prayer For One Who Is Sick

HEAR us, Almighty and most merciful God and Saviour; extend thy accustomed goodness to this thy servant who is grieved with sickness.

Sanctify, we beseech thee, this thy fatherly correction to him; that the sense of his weakness may add strength to his faith, and seriousness to his repentance:

That, if it shall be thy good pleasure to restore him to his former health, he may lead the residue of his life in thy fear, and to thy glory: or else, give him grace so to take thy visitation, that, after this painful life ended, he may dwell with thee in life everlasting; through Jesus Christ our Lord.
Amen.

The Book of Common Prayer,
1662 version

God Of My Life, Look Gently Down

God of my life, look gently down,
Behold the pains I feel;
But I am dumb before Thy throne,
Nor dare dispute Thy will.

Diseases are Thy servants, Lord,
They come at Thy command;
I'll not attempt a murmuring word
Against Thy chastening hand.

Yet I may plead with humble cries,
Remove Thy sharp rebukes;
My strength consumes, my spirit dies,
Through Thy repeated strokes.

Crushed as a moth beneath Thy hand,
We molder to the dust;
Our feeble powers can ne'er withstand,
And all our beauty's lost.

This mortal life decays apace,
How soon the bubble's broke!
Adam and all his numerous race
Are vanity and smoke.

I'm but a sojourner below,
As all my fathers were;
May I be well prepared to go,
When I the summons hear.

But if my life be spared awhile,
Before my last remove,
Thy praise shall be my business still,
And I'll declare Thy love.

Isaac Watts (1674–1748)

Personal Meditation II

LORD, when thou shalt visit me with a sharp disease,
I fear I shall be impatient; for I am choleric by my nature,
and tender by my temper, and have not been acquainted
with sickness all my lifetime. I cannot expect any kind
usage from that which hath been a stranger unto me. I fear
I shall rave and rage. O whither will my mind sail, when
distemper shall steer it? whither will my fancy run, when
diseases shall ride it? My tongue, which of itself is a fire,
sure will be a wildfire, when the furnace of my mouth is
made seven times hotter with a burning fever. But, Lord,
though I should talk idly to my own shame, let me not talk
wickedly to thy dishonour. Teach me the art of patience
whilst I am well, and give me the use of it when I am sick.
In that day either lighten my burden or strengthen my
back. Make me, who so often, in my health, have
discovered my weakness presuming on my own strength,
to be strong in sickness when I solely rely on thy assistance.

Thomas Fuller (1608–61)

For The Health Of Our Bodies

O God the Father of lights, from Whom cometh down every good and perfect gift; Mercifully look upon our frailty and infirmity, and grant us such health of body as Thou knowest to be needful for us; that both in our bodies and souls we may evermore serve Thee with all our strength and might, through Jesus Christ out Lord. Amen.

John Cosin (1594–1672)

The Sickness Unto Death

Father in Heaven! To Thee the congregation often makes its petition for all who are sick and sorrowful, and when someone among us lies ill, alas, of mortal sickness, the congregation sometimes desires a special petition; grant that we may each one of us become in good time aware what sickness it is which is the sickness unto death, and aware that we are all of us suffering from this sickness.

O Lord Jesus Christ, who didst come to earth to heal them that suffer from this sickness, from which, alas, we all suffer, but from which Thou art able to heal only those who are conscious they are sick in this way; help Thou us in this sickness to hold fast to Thee, to the end that we may be healed of it.

O God the Holy Ghost, who comest to help us in this sickness if we honestly desire to be healed; remain with us so that for no single instant we may to our own destruction shun the Physician, but may remain with Him – delivered from sickness. For to be with Him is to be delivered from our sickness, and when we are with Him we are saved from all sickness.

Søren Aabye Kierkegaard (1813–55)

CHILDREN'S
PRAYERS

Now I Lay Me Down To Sleep

Now I lay me down to sleep,
I pray thee, Lord, my soul to keep;
If I should die before I wake,
I pray thee, Lord, my soul to take.

Author unknown, 17th century

Matthew, Mark, Luke And John

Matthew, Mark, Luke and John,
Bless the bed that I lie on.
Four corners to my bed,
Four angels round my head;
One to watch and one to pray
And two to bear my soul away.

Author unknown, traditional

Good-night Prayer For A Little Child

Father, unto Thee I pray,
Thou hast guarded me all day;
Safe I am while in Thy sight,
Safely let me sleep to-night.

Bless my friends, the whole world bless,
Help me to learn helpfulness;
Keep me ever in Thy sight:
So to all I say Good-night.

Henry Johnstone, pre-1907

Child's Evening Hymn

Now the day is over,
　　Night is drawing nigh,
Shadows of the evening
　　Steal across the sky.

Now the darkness gathers,
　　Stars begin to peep,
Birds and beasts and flowers
　　Soon will be asleep.

Jesu, give the weary
　　Calm and sweet repose;
With thy tenderest blessing
　　May our eyelids close.

Grant to little children
　　Visions bright of thee;
Guard the sailors tossing
　　On the deep blue sea.

Comfort every sufferer
　　Watching late in pain;
Those who plan some evil
　　From their sin restrain.

Through the long night-watches
    May thine angels spread
Their white wings above me,
    Watching round my bed.

When the morning wakens,
    Then may I arise
Pure and fresh and sinless
    In thy holy eyes.

Glory to the Father,
    Glory to the Son,
And to thee, bless'd Spirit,
    Whilst all ages run. Amen

Sabine Baring-Gould (1834–1924)

Through The Night Thy Angels Kept

Through the night Thy angels kept
Watch beside me while I slept;
Now the dark has passed away,
Thank Thee, Lord, for this new day.

North and south and east and west
May Thy holy Name be blest;
Everywhere beneath the sun,
As in Heaven, Thy will be done.

Give me food that I may live;
Every naughtiness forgive;
Keep all evil things away
From Thy little child this day.

William Canton (1845–1926)

Jesus, Friend Of Little Children

Jesus, Friend of little children,
Be a friend to me;
Take my hand, and ever keep me
Close to Thee.

Teach me how to grow in goodness,
Daily as I grow;
Thou hast been a child, and surely
Thou dost know.

Step by step O lead me onward,
Upward into youth;
Wiser, stronger, still becoming
In Thy truth.

Never leave me, nor forsake me;
Ever be my friend;
For I need Thee, from life's dawning
To its end.

Walter John Mathams (1853–1931)

Refrain From 'Jesus Loves The Little Children'

Jesus loves the little children,
All the children of the world.
Red and yellow, black and white,
All are precious in his sight,
Jesus loves the little children of the world.

Clare Herbert Woolston (1856–1927)

Gentle Jesus, Meek And Mild

Gentle Jesus, meek and mild,
Look upon a little child;
Pity my simplicity,
Suffer me to come to Thee.

Fain I would to Thee be brought,
Dearest God, forbid it not;
Give me, dearest God, a place
In the kingdom of Thy grace.

Lamb of God, I look to Thee;
Thou shalt my Example be;
Thou art gentle, meek, and mild;
Thou wast once a little child.

Fain I would be as Thou art;
Give me Thine obedient heart;
Thou art pitiful and kind,
Let me have Thy loving mind.

Let me, above all, fulfil
God my heav'nly Father's will;
Never His good Spirit grieve;
Only to His glory live.

Thou didst live to God alone;
Thou didst never seek Thine own;
Thou Thyself didst never please:
God was all Thy happiness.

Loving Jesus, gentle Lamb,
In Thy gracious hands I am;
Make me, Saviour, what Thou art,
Live Thyself within my heart.

I shall then show forth Thy praise,
Serve Thee all my happy days;
Then the world shall always see
Christ, the holy Child, in me.

Charles Wesley (1707–88)

Be Near Me, Lord Jesus

Be near me, Lord Jesus,
    I ask Thee to stay
Close by me forever,
    and love me, I pray.
Bless all the dear children
    in thy tender care,
And fit us for heaven,
    to live with Thee there.

The third stanza from Away in
A Manger. *First printed in 1892,
probably by Charles Hutchinson
Gabriel (1856–1932), or possibly
John McFarland*

A Simple Thanksgiving Prayer

For each new morning with its light,
For rest and shelter of the night,
For health and food, for love and friends,
For everything Thy goodness sends.

Ralph Waldo Emerson (1803–82)

Jesus Loves Me

Jesus loves me – this I know,
For the Bible tells me so,
Little ones to Him belong,
They are weak but He is strong.
Yes, Jesus loves me.
Yes, Jesus loves me.
Yes, Jesus loves me. The Bible tells me so.

Anna Bartlett Warner (1827–1915)

Lead Us, Heavenly Father

Lead us, heavenly Father,
In our opening way,
Lead us in the morning
Of our little day.
While our hearts are happy,
While our souls are free,
May we give our childhood
As a song to Thee.

Lead us, heavenly Father,
As the way grows long,
Be our strong salvation,
Be our joyous song.
Gladdened by Thy mercies,
Chastened by Thy rod,
May we walk through all things
Humbly with our God.

Lead us, heavenly Father,
By Thy voices clear –
Through Thy prophets holy,
Through Thy Son so dear –
Him Who took the children
In His arms of love;
May we all be gathered
In His home above.

Brooke Herford (∂. c. 1903)

Father In Heaven…

Father in heaven,
Help Thy little children
To love and serve Thee
Throughout this day.
Help us to be truthful
Help us to be kindly.
That we may please Thee
In all we do or say. Amen.

Kate Douglas Wiggin (1856–1923)

Child's Grace

Thank you God for
  the world so sweet,
Thank you for the
  food we eat,
Thank you for the
  birds that sing
Thank you, God, for
  everything!

Edith Rutter Leatham
(19th–20th century)

Lord And Saviour, True And Kind

Lord and Saviour, true and kind,
Be the Master of my mind;
Bless, and guide, and strengthen still
All my powers of thought and will.

While I ply the scholar's task,
Jesus Christ, be near, I ask;
Help the memory, clear the brain,
Knowledge still to seek and gain.

Here I train for life's swift race;
Let me do it in Thy grace;
Here I arm me for life's fight;
Let me do it in Thy might.

Thou hast made me mind and soul;
I for Thee would use the whole;
Thou hast died that I might live;
All my powers to Thee I give.

Striving, thinking, learning, still,
Let me follow thus Thy will,
Till my whole glad nature be
Trained for duty and for Thee.

Handley Carr Glynn Moule (1841–1920)

313

Picture Credits

All pictures are courtesy of the Fine Art Photographic Library.

5, 180 Charles Rolt (*fl.* 1845–67), *The Sermon On The Mount*

6, 47 Rudolf Von Alt (1812–1905), *The Interior of St Peter's Basilica, Rome, Italy,* 1836

7, 282–283 Joseph Clark (1834–1926), *Favourite Fruits*

9, 190 William Banks Fortescue (d. 1924), *Gift House Bretheren*

10–11 George Lance (1802–64), *Nature's Bounty*

12 Hubert and Jan Van Eyck (*c.* 1400), *God, the Father*

15 Evelyn de Morgan (1855–1919), *Tobias and the Angel,* 1875

19 Faustin (1847–*c.* 1914), *April Showers Bring May Flowers*

20–27 Carl Frederic Aagaard (1833–95), *A Forest Glade*

28–31 Jose Y Arnosa Gallegos (1859–1917), *Mass*

32 Joseph Clark (1834–1926), *A Family Gathering*

35 Anonymous, *Carol Singing*

37 George Law Beetholme (*fl.* 1847–78), *A Romantic Landscape With Waterfall*

38–41 Thomas Bolton Gilchrist Dalziel (1823–1906), *The Abating Storm*

42 Anonymous, *The Carol Singers*

44–45 Giovanni Falchetti (1843–1918), *A Still Life Of Fruit*

51 Anonymous, *Glory, Glory In The Highest, Unto God & Peace On Earth*

52–53 Walter Langley (1852–1922), *Getting Better*

54 Bennozzo Di Gozzoli, *Adoration Of The Shepherds*

55–56 Giovanni-Battista Gaulli (1639–1709), *The Adoration Of The Golden Calf, With Moses And Mount Sinai*

60 Joshua Hargrave Sams Mann (*fl.* 1849–84), *The New Arrival*

63 Gustave Doré (1832–83), *The Wave*

68–69 Louis-Emile Adan (1839–1937), *La Maternité*

71–73 Samuel Lawson Booth (1836–1928), *Jerusalem The Golden (Israel)*

74–76 Hubert & Jan Van Eyck (*c.* 1400), *St Cecilia Playing The Organ*

78 Henry H. Parker (1858–1930), *Harvesting Corn*

82 Sir Edward Coley Burne-Jones (1833–98), *Santa Maria Virgo*

85 Hubert & Jan Van Eyck (*c.* 1400), *A Choir Of Angels*

86 Knut Ekwall (1843–1912), *Consolation*

88–89, 320 Cristoforo Da Bologna (15th cent.), *Descent From The Cross*

90 Jean-Marie Berthelier (b. 1834), *A Still Life Of Fruit*

92–94 Mary Evelina Kindon (*fl.* 1879–1918), *Saying Grace*

95 Edmund Swift, *Saying Grace,* 1868

96–97 Joseph Clark (1834–1926), *The Christmas Pudding*

100–01 Mary Helen Shaw (d. 1911), *Faith Hope and Charity,* 1903

102–03 Angelus De Baets (1793–1855), *Ghent Cathedral, Belgium*

104 Paul Madeline (1863–1920), *Pins Au Bord De La Mer*

107 Sir Joseph Noel Paton (1821–1901), *The Valley Of The Shadow Of Death,* 1866

108–11 Helen Allingham (1848–1926), *A Cottage Near Witley, Surrey, England*

112 Frederick Daniel Hardy (1826–1911), *Vesper Bells,* 1894

114–15 Edward Henry Corbould (1815–1905), *The Warhorse*

116–17 Albert Gabriel Rigolot (1862–1932), *Hazy Sunshine (Sunset)*

119 Alfred Augustus Glendening (1861–1907), *A Spring Morning*

120 Anonymous (19/20th cent.), *The Angel's Message*

Acknowledgments

All extracts from *The Book of Common Prayer* (1662 version), the rights in which are vested in the Crown, are reproduced by permission of the Crown's Patentee, Cambridge University Press.

Thanks to Alan Scott Wesemann for permission to reproduce his *A Thanksgiving Day Prayer* (page 98).

Thanks to Pax Christi UK for permission to reproduce prayers from their website: *Pax Christi Daily Prayer* (page 210) and *An Interfaith Prayer for Peace* (page 228).

Every effort has been made to contact copyright holders and to obtain permission where appropriate. In the event of an oversight the publishers would be glad to rectify any omissions in future editions of this book.

Index of Titles

Index of Authors or Sources